Editor
Heather Douglas

Illustrator
Kelly McMahon

Editor in Chief
Ina Massler Levin, M.A.

Creative Director
Karen J. Goldfluss, M.S. Ed.

Cover Artist
Barb Lorseyedi

Art Coordinator
Renée Mc Elwee

Imaging
Leonard P. Swierski

ITSY BITSY STORIES
for Reading Comprehension

Short, high-interest stories that promote fluency, comprehension, and vocabulary development!

Teacher Created Resources

Publisher

Mary D. Smith, M.S. Ed.

Author

Susan Mackey Collins, M.Ed.

Teacher Created Resources
12621 Western Avenue
Garden Grove, CA 92841
www.teachercreated.com
ISBN: 978-1-4206-3265-1

©2011 Teacher Created Resources
Reprinted, 2016
Made in U.S.A.

Table of Contents

Introduction

Reading is the foundation for all education. Practicing and exposing a child to a variety of reading opportunities is key to creating a successful reader. *Itsy Bitsy Stories for Reading Comprehension, Grade K*, does just that.

Itsy Bitsy Stories for Reading Comprehension, Grade K, is the perfect supplement to any reading program. The activities in this book are geared towards providing a variety of educational and entertaining fictional stories. These stories are short yet provide a high interest level for the reader. The activities in this book can be used successfully by any teacher in the regular classroom. The activities can also be used as homework to reinforce skills taught during the school day. This book has been written to help teach and reinforce important reading skills such as fluency, comprehension, and vocabulary. Teachers are sure to find a variety of ways to use this book in their classrooms.

Another feature with each reading passage in *Itsy Bitsy Stories for Reading Comprehension, Grade K*, is the "Something Extra" activities which follow each story. For the teacher wishing to extend each reading opportunity, these activities provide yet another way to engage students even further in the joy of reading.

More Ideas for Teachers and Parents on How to Make the Most of This Book:

- Read aloud some of the stories.

- Have each student practice some of the activities on his or her own.

- Focus on key vocabulary words and take note of any words a students still needs to practice and learn.

- Review any work the student does on his or her own.

- Extend lessons by assigning extra stories for students who are ready to move forward.

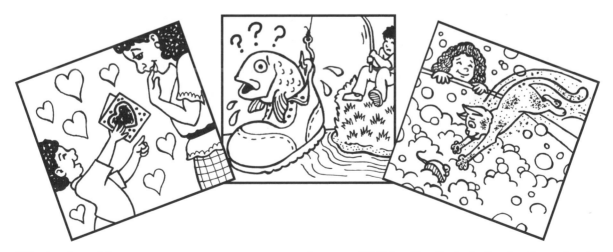

Let's Go!

"It is time for the trip," Mom said.

"It is time to go," Dad said.

We get in the car. We like to go.
We want to go on the trip.

"Let's go," I said.

"We can't go," Mom said.

"We can't go," Dad said.

"Why can't we go?" I said.

"We forgot the keys!"

1. Which word has the same beginning sound as the word "<u>tr</u>ip"?

   a. tick

   b. top

   c. truck

2. Who is going on a trip?

   a. Mom, Dad, and child

   b. Mom and Dad

   c. Mom

3. Why can't they go on the trip?

   a. They forgot the car.

   b. They forgot the dog.

   c. They forgot the keys.

Something extra: Where would you like to go on a trip? On the back of this page, draw and color a picture of a place you would like to go.

The Farmer Says Good Night

"Oink, oink, oink," said the pig.

"Moo, moo, moo," said the cow.

"Quack, quack, quack," said the duck.

"Woof, woof, woof," said the dog.

"Hush, hush, hush," said the farmer. "It is time to go to bed!"

1. What does the cow say?

    a. quack

    b. moo

    c. hush

2. When do most people go to bed?

    a. at night

    b. at breakfast

    c. at noon

3. The farmer is ready to go to

    a. the barn.

    b. his bed.

    c. the store.

Something extra: On the back of the page, draw and color a picture of your favorite animal. Write the name of your animal. What sound does it make?

_____

My animal: _____

_____

It makes this sound: _____

A Card for Mom

I made a card. It is for my mom. I will give it to her.   Mom likes to get cards from me. She will like this card. It is special. It has a heart on it. It says I love her.

I love my mom. My mom loves me.

1. In the story, Mom likes

    a. candy.

    b. cards.

    c. rings.

2. What shape is on the card?

    a. a heart

    b. a square

    c. a diamond

3. What word has the same beginning sound as the word "card"?

    a. heart

    b. cat

    c. chair

Something extra: Get a piece of paper from your teacher. Make a card and give it to someone special. Write the name of your special person:

_____

- -

_____

I Can Help

Mom wants to bake a cake. I will help her. I will get the eggs. I will get the oil. I will help her stir. We will bake the cake. We will watch it cook. It is great to help mom bake. What is the best part? When we get to eat the cake.

---

1. What does Mom want to bake?

    a. a pie

    b. a cookie

    c. a cake

2. What is needed to bake the cake?

    a. eggs and oil

    b. bacon and eggs

    c. oil and bread

3. Which word rhymes with cake?

    a. snake

    b. star

    c. pup

Something extra: Make your own cake. On the back of this page, draw and color a picture of your own cake. Pretend the cake is for your birthday.

Playing Together

"I have a new ball. I like to play ball. I want to play. Who will play with me?" said the girl.

"I have a new bat. I like to play ball. I want to play. I will play with you," said the boy.

"We have a ball. We have a bat. We like to play. We want to play. We will play together," said the girl and boy.

1. The girl has a

   a. glove.

   b. ball.

   c. bat.

2. Choose the answer that shows two bats.

   a.

   b.

   c.

3. Which word has the same beginning sound as the word "ball"?

   a. tub

   b. doll

   c. bag

Something extra: What game do you like to play? On the back of the page, draw and color a picture of the game you like to play.

The Wish Box

Pip found a red box. Pip took the box to his mom. She said it was a special box. It was a wish box. She told Pip to make a wish. Pip did. He opened the box. It was empty.

"What did you wish for?" she said.

"I wished for a hug from you!"

Pip smiled. His wish came true.

---

1. What color is the box?

   a. green

   b. blue

   c. red

2. What is the box?

   a. a wish box

   b. a gift box

   c. a shoe box

3. What is Pip's wish?

   a. a new toy

   b. a hug

   c. an ice–cream cone

Something extra: Everyone likes wishes. What would you wish for if you could? Write your three wishes on the lines.

1. _____

_____

2. _____

_____

3. _____

Is It Time?

Is it time? Is it time? All the birds want to know.

Mother Bird sings this song. "I had three eggs. Now there are three baby birds. It is time! It is time!"

Mother Bird sings her song. Three baby birds sing with her.

---

1. What time is it?

   a. time to eat

   b. time for the baby birds

   c. time to sleep

2. How many baby birds are there?

   a. 1

   b. 2

   c. 3

3. Who sings with Mother Bird?

   a. one baby bird

   b. two baby birds

   c. three baby birds

Something extra: Most people like music. What is your favorite song?

- -

Why do you like this song?

- -

Do you like to sing?

- -

Kate Can Skate

Kate wants to skate. Kate will not let go of her dad's hand. Her dad tells her she can skate. He smiles at her. Kate lets go. Kate smiles. She is skating!

1. What does Kate want to do?

   a. swim

   b. skate

   c. run

2. How does Kate feel when she skates?

   a.

   b.

   c.

3. Which word has the same beginning sound as the word "skate"?

   a. snake

   b. skunk

   c. sun

Something extra: Kate wears a helmet to be safe. Color something else in the picture at the top of the page that helps keep Kate safe.

Everyone Can Share

Dan likes to play with cars. Sam likes to play with blocks. Sam makes a road with his blocks. Dan gives Sam a car. Dan and Sam play with the blocks. Dan and Sam play with the cars. Dan and Sam think sharing is fun.

1. Dan likes to play with

   a. blocks.

   b. cars.

   c. balls.

2. Sam likes to play with

   a. blocks.

   b. cars.

   c. tops.

3. Sam and Dan like to

   a. share.

   b. eat.

   c. sleep.

Something extra: List three things you can share.

1. _____

2. _____

3. _____

The Surprise Catch

Bob likes to fish. He has a pole. He has a worm. He has a hook. Bob has a bite! What is on the hook? Bob has a shoe. There is a shoe on the hook. What is in the shoe? A fish is in the shoe! Bob lets the fish go. What a lucky fish!

1. What does Bob like to do?

    a. swim

    b. skate

    c. fish

2. What is on Bob's <u>hook</u>?

    a. a fish

    b. a shoe

    c. a can

3. Why is the fish lucky?

    a. He is set free.

    b. He can swim.

    c. He is in the shoe.

Something extra: The fish in the story is lucky. Has anything lucky happened to you? On the back of the page, draw and color a picture of a time when something lucky happened to you.

Max Rides

Max rides the bus. The bus ride is fun. The bus goes up the hill. The bus goes down the hill. Max likes to ride the bus.

On the weekend Max does not ride the bus. That is when Max rides his bike. Max rides his bike up the hill. Max rides his bike down the hill. Max likes to ride!

1. What does Max ride?

   a. a car and a bus

   b. a bus and a truck

   c. a bus and a bike

2. The bus goes _____ and

_____ the hill.

   a. up *and* across

   b. across *and* down

   c. up *and* down

3. What does Max like to do?

   a. ride

   b. run

   c. hop

Something extra: List three things that go up and down.

1. _____

2. _____

3. _____

My Dad and the Sea

My dad lives at the sea. I go and see my dad. We play in the sand. We use my pail. We make hills in the sand. We make big hills. We make small hills. The waves take the hills away. Then we make more.

1. Where does the story take place?

    a. the city

    b. a farm

    c. the sea

2. What word has the same beginning sound as the word "pail"?

    a. pan

    b. bucket

    c. water

3. What do the girl and her dad like to do?

    a. play in the water

    b. play inside

    c. play in the sand

Something extra: List three things you can do at the beach.

1. _____

2. _____

3. _____

At the Farm

I see a duck. I see a chick. I see a turkey. I see the birds down at the farm.

The duck sees me. The chick sees me. The turkey sees me. The birds see me down at the farm.

1. Where are the birds?

    a. at the zoo

    b. at the woods

    c. at the farm

2. How many kinds of birds are in the story?

    a. 1

    b. 2

    c. 3

3. Where does the story take place?

    a. the farm

    b. the sea

    c. the woods

Something extra: The story tells about three birds. List or draw three more types of birds.

1. _____

2. _____

3. _____

The Tiny Seed

Pat eats a pear. She finds a seed.
She wants a pear tree. She plants
the seed in the dirt. Pat gives the
seed water. One day Pat sees a
green plant in the dirt. The seed
will soon be a tree!

1. What does Pat find?

   a. a plant

   b. a pear

   c. a seed

2. What does Pat want?

   a. an apple tree

   b. a peach tree

   c. a pear tree

3. What will the seed become?

   a. a flower

   b. a tree

   c. a plant

Something extra: Make your own fruit. Put together the names of two fruits you know and make a new fruit.

Example: pear and banana = pearana

On the back of this page, be sure to draw and color a picture of the new fruit.

fruit 1: _____

fruit 2: _____

new fruit: _____

Where Is Teddy?

Ken wants a nap. Where is his teddy bear? He looks on the floor. He looks in his room. No bear. He gets in bed. What is at his toes? His bear is in bed!

1. What does Ken want to do?

   a. go outside

   b. go to bed

   c. go to school

2. Where is the bear?

   a. on the floor

   b. in the bed

   c. under the bed

3. Which word has the same beginning sound as "nap"?

   a. net

   b. map

   c. hat

Something extra: Below or on the back of this page, draw and color a picture of Ken's teddy bear.

Get It Clean

Jess's room is not clean. Jess needs to clean his room. Jess does not think it is fun to clean. His dad comes in his room. He starts to sing. Jess starts to sing. His dad starts to clean. Jess starts to clean. They clean and sing. They sing and clean. Jess's dad hugs him. Jess looks at his room. It is clean! Cleaning with his dad is lots of fun.

1. What does Jess need to clean?

   a. his ears

   b. his shoes

   c. his room

2. What do Jess and his dad do?

   a. talk and clean

   b. sing and clean

   c. play and clean

3. Jess thinks the job was

   a. hard.

   b. sad.

   c. fun.

Something extra: List three things you can do while you sing.

1. _____

2. _____

3. _____

Whirl and Twirl

Gage likes to spin. He spins and spins. He falls down. He gets up. He spins again. It is fun to whirl and twirl.

1. What does Gage like to do?

    a. dance

    b. swim

    c. spin

2. Sometimes Gage falls

    a. up.

    b. down.

    c. across.

3. Which word has the same beginning sound as the word "whirl"?

    a. whale

    b. fish

    c. frog

Something extra: Gage likes to whirl and twirl. List three things you like to do.

1. _____

2. _____

3. _____

Muddy Fun

Kip wants to make mud pies. He has dirt. He has no water. How can Kip make mud pies? The sky gets dark. Kip runs in. The rain comes. The rain stops. Kip runs out. Kip can make mud pies!

1. What does Kip need to make his pies?

   a. water

   b. eggs

   c. sugar

2. How does Kip get water?

   a. from a glass

   b. from the rain

   c. from the creek

3. Kip likes to play

   a. in his room.

   b. outside.

   c. at school.

Something extra: List three ways you can get water.

1. _____

2. _____

3. _____

Jump and Jump

Mary loves to jump. She jumps on clouds. She jumps on planes. She jumps and jumps.

Mary wakes up. It was all a dream! She smiles. She knows what she can do. She can jump rope!

---

1. What does Mary like to do?

   a. skip

   b. run

   c. jump

2. Mary is going to go

   a. jumping.

   b. skating.

   c. walking.

3. Which word rhymes with the word "dream"?

   a. team

   b. day

   c. jump

Something extra: Everyone has dreams. List three things you have dreamed about.

1. _____

2. _____

3. _____

A Nice View

Meg gets a pet bird. She sets the bird's cage on a table. Her bird does not sing. Meg moves the cage. She sets the bird's cage on a chair. Her bird does not sing. Meg moves the cage. She sets the bird's cage by the window. Meg's bird sings and sings.

1. In the story, the bird lives in a
   a. box.
   b. shoe.
   c. cage.

2. Where is the bird happy?
   a. on the table
   b. on the chair
   c. by the window

3. How does Meg know her bird is happy?
   a. It sings.
   b. It flies.
   c. It eats.

Something extra: What makes you happy? List three things that make you happy.

1. _____

2. _____

3. _____

A Little Help

Once there was an inchworm. He was very sad.

"Why are you sad?" said his mom.

"I am too small," he said.

His mom sat by him. She held one of his hands.

"Together we are two inches long!"

The inchworm was happy. He felt so tall and so loved!

---

1. Why is the inchworm sad?

    a. He is too tall.

    b. He is too small.

    c. He is too shy.

2. Who helps the inchworm?

    a. his friend

    b. his dad

    c. his mom

3. Why is the inchworm happy?

    a. He feels taller.

    b. He feels loved.

    c. both a and b

Something extra: In the space below, draw and color a picture of you as an inchworm!

A Special Quilt

Jade loved her quilt. Her mom had made the quilt for Jade. One day Jade could not find the quilt. Jade looked all over the place. Then she saw her dad. He was asleep. Dad had the quilt. Jade was glad Dad liked the quilt, too.

1. Who made Jade's quilt?

   a. her dad

   b. her grandmother

   c. her mom

2. Who had Jade's quilt?

   a. her mom

   b. her dad

   c. her dog

3. Which word has the same beginning sound as the word "quilt"?

   a. queen

   b. king

   c. blanket

Something extra: On the back of this page, draw and color your own quilt. Make sure the quilt has a pattern or picture.

The Music Box

Cam loved his mom's music box. It was made of wood and glass. Cam loved the song it played. His mom would sing the song. Cam would sing with her. The music would stop. Cam's mom would wind up the box. They would sing some more.

1. What is a music box?

   a. a box that plays music

   b. a box that plays games

   c. a box that plays movies

2. The box is made of wood and

   a. clay.

   b. glass.

   c. metal.

3. What did Cam and his mom do together?

   a. sing

   b. dance

   c. skip

Something extra: List three things you do with someone at your house.

1. _____

   _____

2. _____

   _____

3. _____

Cut and Glue

Ann cuts the page. Bill likes to glue. Bill adds red and blue paper to the page. Ann and Bill make a picture. They hang it on the wall. Ann and Bill start again. Ann and Bill like to cut and glue.

1. What does Bill like to do?

   a. color

   b. cut

   c. glue

2. Where do Ann and Bill hang their picture?

   a. on the door

   b. on the floor

   c. on the wall

3. Which word has the same <u>ending</u> sound as the word "glue"?

   a. blue

   b. green

   c. red

Something extra: What are your favorite colors?

_____

My favorite colors: _____

_____

On the back of the page, draw and color a picture using only your favorite colors.

Who Is Sleeping?

The sun came up. The moon went down. It is time for a new day. "Get up! Get up!" all of the birds said. One bird did not get up. Who is asleep? The owl is asleep. He has played all night. He will sleep today. The sun will go down. The moon will go up. Then owl will start his day!

1. How do the birds know it is daytime?

    a. The sun came up.

    b. The sun went down.

    c. There is no sun.

2. Who is asleep?

    a. the deer

    b. the skunk

    c. the owl

3. When is owl awake?

    a. at night

    b. in the day

    c. all the time

Something extra: List three things you do at night.

1. _____

2. _____

3. _____

Funny Little Dog

Tim's dog likes to play. Tim's dog chews on his shoes. The dog does not play with his toys. Tim gives the dog a shoe. The dog plays and plays. What a funny little dog!

1. What does Tim give his dog?

   a. a bone

   b. a stick

   c. a shoe

2. What does Tim's dog like to do with a shoe?

   a. chew on it

   b. run with it

   c. hide it

3. Which word has the same <u>ending</u> sound as the word "dog"?

   a. shoe

   b. log

   c. tub

Something extra: Tim's dog likes to chew on shoes. List three things you like to chew! (Now who's the funny puppy?)

1. _____

_____

2. _____

_____

3. _____

Fun Being Dan

Dan wants to be a bear. Dan tries to growl. He tries to stomp. He tries to be a bear. Dan looks in the mirror. He is not a bear.

Dan's mother calls for Dan. She has an ice–cream cone for him. Dan looks in the mirror again. He is glad he is not a bear. Bears do not get to eat ice cream. Dan is glad he is a boy.

1. What does Dan wish he could be?

    a. a tiger

    b. an owl

    c. a bear

2. What does Dan see in the mirror?

    a. Dan

    b. a bear

    c. ice cream

3. Who gives Dan the ice cream?

    a. the bear

    b. Dan's teacher

    c. Dan's mom

Something extra: Dan likes ice cream. Think of a new kind of ice cream. Then write the steps needed to make the ice cream. Use the back of the paper if you need more space.

Ice cream flavor: _____

How to make the new flavor of ice cream: _____

What's Popping?

Farmer Brown looks at his corn. The day is hot. The corn is hot.

Pop! Pop! Pop!

The corn is popping!

Farmer Brown gets a bag. He gets some butter. He sits down. He has a good snack.

---

1. Which food does Farmer Brown see?

   a. beans

   b. pumpkins

   c. corn

2. What happens to Farmer Brown's corn?

   a. It is missing.

   b. It is growing.

   c. It is popping.

3. What sound does the corn make?

   a. splat

   b. ping

   c. pop

Something extra: Lots of things make noises. List three things that make noise. Write the noise each one makes.

1. _____   noise: _____

2. _____   noise: _____

3. _____   noise: _____

The Blue Coat

Pam has a blue raincoat. She loves her coat. She wears it outside to play in the rain. Pam wants to play in the rain. She cannot find her coat. Her mom has her coat. She has washed her coat. She helps Pam put on her blue coat. Now it is time to play.

1. What color is Pam's raincoat?

    a. green

    b. white

    c. blue

2. Who has Pam's coat?

    a. her dad

    b. her sister

    c. her mom

3. What does Pam do outside?

    a. play

    b. read

    c. sit

Something extra: The word *raincoat* is made of two words: *rain* and *coat*. List three more words made from two or more words.

1. _____

2. _____

3. _____

Lucky Jay

Jay wants to make a wish. Jay
looks at the sky. There are no stars.
The sky is dark. There is no star
to make a wish. Jay looks down.
There is a clover with four leaves.
Jay does not need a wish now. He
has a lucky clover.

1. What does Jay need to make his
   wish?

   a. a star

   b. a rabbit

   c. the moon

2. What does Jay find?

   a. a star

   b. a clover

   c. a penny

3. Why does Jay like the clover?

   a. It is pretty.

   b. It is lucky.

   c. It is funny.

Something extra: Below or on the back of the page, draw and color a night sky
for Jay. Have a lot of stars in the sky.

A Wonderful View

Sadie likes clouds. She likes to look at clouds. She sees shapes in the clouds. She sees fish. She sees clowns. She sees camels. She sees all this in the sky. Sadie can't wait to look at more clouds. What will she see the next time she looks?

1. What does Sadie like?

    a. cows

    b. clowns

    c. clouds

2. Why does Sadie like clouds?

    a. She talks to them.

    b. She hides under them.

    c. She sees shapes in them.

3. Which one is a shape Sadie sees?

    a. a camel

    b. a pig

    c. a dog

Something extra: With your teacher's or parents' okay, take your paper outside. Look at the clouds. List three shapes you see in the clouds.

1. _____

2. _____

3. _____

Baby and Me

Mom had a baby. His name is Jay.
I want to play with Jay. Jay cannot
play. He is too small. Jay can
smile at me. I like his smile. I smile
back. He smiles at me. Jay can
play! I like this game.

---

1. Why can't the baby play?

    a. He is too shy.

    b. He is too small.

    c. He is too big.

2. How does Jay begin to play?

    a. He runs.

    b. He sings.

    c. He smiles.

3. A good title for this story could be

    a. *Baby Starts to Play*

    b. *I Like Babies*

    c. *The Baby Sleeps*

Something extra: Jay is very small. He is too little to do some things. List three things you are too little to do.

1. _____

2. _____

3. _____

Dot Can't Sleep

Dot can't sleep. Tick tock. Tick tock. The clock is too loud. Dot shuts her eyes. Tick tock. Tick tock. Dot gets out of bed. Dot sets the clock in the hall. She shuts her door. No tick tock. All is quiet. Dot can sleep.

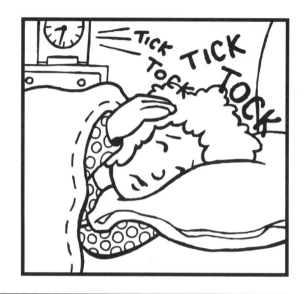

1. Why can't Dot sleep?

    a. A dog is barking.

    b. A clock is ticking.

    c. A man is talking.

2. What sound does the clock make?

    a. splish splash

    b. bang bang

    c. tick tock

3. Which word has the same <u>ending</u> sound as the word "clock"?

    a. sock

    b. shoe

    c. cake

Something extra: Look around the room. List three things in the room that are very <u>quiet</u>.

1. _____

2. _____

3. _____

Bear Eats Some Honey

Bear wants to eat. He likes honey. The bees give bear a cup of honey. It is sweet. It is good. Bear is glad the bees are his friends.

1. What does Bear want to eat?

   a. an apple

   b. pizza

   c. honey

2. Why do the bees give Bear food?

   a. The bees like Bear.

   b. The bees do not like Bear.

   c. The bees are hungry.

3. Who is the main character in the story?

   a. the bees

   b. the honey

   c. the bear

Something extra: What food do you like best? Below or on the back of this page, draw and color a picture of your favorite food.

A Guest for Tea

Miss Mouse is having tea. There will be food and drink. Miss Cat wishes she could go. Miss Cat wants some food.

Miss Mouse is kind. She tells Miss Cat to come to tea. Miss Mouse is smart. She tells Miss Cat to wear her party gloves. The gloves will cover her sharp claws. The food and tea will keep her mouth full.

Miss Cat was a "purrfect" guest!

1. Miss Cat is

   a. cold.

   b. hot.

   c. hungry.

2. What does Miss Cat wear to the tea party?

   a. boots

   b. gloves

   c. rings

3. What does the word "purrfect" mean?

   a. bad

   b. mean

   c. good

Something extra: Miss Cat is so hungry. What food would you want if you were hungry? Write a list below or draw pictures on the back of this page of foods you would want to eat.

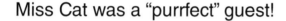

List: _____

_____

_____

What a Surprise!

Mike has a loose tooth. It will not come out. He eats an apple. It does not come out. He eats some taffy. It does not come out. He chews some gum. It does not come out.

Mike wants to eat. He gets a piece of bread. He takes a bite. He cannot believe it. Out pops his tooth!

---

1. What does Mike eat first?

    a. taffy

    b. bread

    c. apple

2. What does Mike eat last?

    a. apple

    b. bread

    c. taffy

3. What does Mike lose?

    a. his toy

    b. his shoes

    c. his tooth

Something extra: List three things you do not want to ever lose.

1. _____

_____

2. _____

_____

3. _____

Kim's Great Idea

Kim's cat is not clean. Her cat needs a bath. Her cat will not get in the tub. Kim has an idea. She puts a toy mouse in the water. The cat jumps in the tub. Kim's great idea works!

1. Who needs a bath?

    a. Kim

    b. the mouse

    c. the cat

2. What is Kim's great idea?

    a. She gives the cat a mouse.

    b. She gives the cat a fish.

    c. She gives the cat a ball.

3. Which word rhymes with "cat"?

    a. hat

    b. tub

    c. dog

Something extra: Put the pictures below in order. Write 1 under the picture that is first. Write 2 under the picture that is second. Write 3 under the picture that is third. Color the pictures when you are done.

_____   _____   _____

- - - - - - -   - - - - - - -   - - - - - - -

_____   _____   _____

The Lost Ring

Kit liked to climb her tree. It started to rain. She went inside. Kit's mom saw her ring was gone! The sun came out. Kit went up in the tree again. The ring was on a branch. She found her ring!

1. What does Kit like to climb?

   a. ladders

   b. stairs

   c. trees

2. Why does Kit go inside?

   a. It is snowing.

   b. It is dark.

   c. It is raining.

3. What does Kit find?

   a. her ring

   b. her book

   c. her coat

Something extra: The word "ring" begins with the letter "r". Write four more words that begin with the letter "r".

1. _____

2. _____

3. _____

4. _____

Up, Up, and Away

Lane has a balloon. He writes a note. He ties the note to the string. He lets it go. It goes up in the sky. Up, up, and away it goes. Who will find the note? Lane does not know. Lane hopes it goes far, far away.

1. What does Lane tie to the string?

    a. a feather

    b. a flower

    c. a note

2. Where does the note go?

    a. to a mailbox

    b. up in the sky

    c. to Lane's house

3. Where does Lane want the note to go?

    a. far away

    b. Lane's house

    c. in his mailbox

Something extra: Below or on the back of this paper, write a short note to a friend. Tell the friend about your day.

_____

- -

_____

- -

_____

- -

Busy, Busy

Snip! Snip! Tad snips the paper.

Snap! Snap! Tad snaps a stick.

Pop! Pop! Tad pops the gum.

Ring! Ring! Tad rings a bell.

Zip! Zip! Tad zips the zipper.

Zzzz! Zzzz! Tad is asleep.

1. What would Tad use to snip the paper?

    a. glue

    b. crayons

    c. scissors

2. What goes "pop"?

    a. the zipper

    b. the bell

    c. the gum

3. What does Tad ring?

    a. the stick

    b. the gum

    c. the bell

Something extra: What is something else Tad can do?

Write one more line for the story.

_____

- -

_____

- -

_____

Answer Sheets

Student Name: _____

Title of Reading Passage: _____

1. (a) (b) (c)

2. (a) (b) (c)

3. (a) (b) (c)

Student Name: _____

Title of Reading Passage: _____

1. (a) (b) (c)

2. (a) (b) (c)

3. (a) (b) (c)

Answer Key

Page 4: Let's Go!
1. c
2. a
3. c

Page 5: What Do you See?
1. c
2. a
3. b

Page 6: I Wish I Could
1. b
2. b
3. a

Page 7: The Farmer Says Good Night
1. b
2. a
3. b

Page 8: A Card for Mom
1. b
2. a
3. b

Page 9: I Can Help
1. c
2. a
3. a

Page 10: Playing Together
1. b
2. a
3. c

Page 11: The Wish Box
1. c
2. a
3. b

Page 12: Is It Time?
1. b
2. c
3. c

Page 13: Kate Can Skate
1. b
2. c
3. b

Page 14: Everyone Can Share
1. b
2. a
3. a

Page 15: The Surprise Catch
1. c
2. b
3. a

Page 16: Max Rides
1. c
2. c
3. a

Page 17: My Dad and the Sea
1. c
2. a
3. c

Page 18: At the Farm
1. c
2. c
3. a

Page 19: The Tiny Seed
1. c
2. c
3. b

Page 20: Where Is Teddy?
1. b
2. b
3. a

Page 21: Get It Clean
1. c
2. b
3. c

Page 22: Whirl and Twirl
1. c
2. b
3. a

Page 23: Muddy Fun
1. a
2. b
3. b

Page 24: Jump and Jump
1. c
2. a
3. a

Page 25: A Nice View
1. c
2. c
3. a

Answer Key *(cont.)*

Page 26: A Little Help
1. b
2. c
3. c

Page 27: A Special Quilt
1. c
2. b
3. a

Page 28: The Music Box
1. a
2. b
3. a

Page 29: Cut and Glue
1. c
2. c
3. a

Page 30: Who Is Sleeping?
1. a
2. c
3. a

Page 31: Funny Little Dog
1. c
2. a
3. b

Page 32: Fun Being Dan
1. c
2. a
3. c

Page 33: What's Popping?
1. c
2. c
3. c

Page 34: The Blue Coat
1. c
2. c
3. a

Page 35: Lucky Jay
1. a
2. b
3. b

Page 36: A Wonderful View
1. c
2. c
3. a

Page 37: Baby and Me
1. b
2. c
3. a

Page 38: Dot Can't Sleep
1. b
2. c
3. a

Page 39: Bear Eats Some Honey
1. c
2. a
3. c

Page 40: A Guest for Tea
1. c
2. b
3. c

Page 41: What a Surprise!
1. c
2. b
3. c

Page 42: Kim's Great Idea
1. c
2. a
3. a

Page 43: The Lost Ring
1. c
2. c
3. a

Page 44: Up, Up, and Away
1. c
2. b
3. a

Page 45: Busy, Busy
1. c
2. c
3. c

Made in the USA
Thornton, CO
11/11/22 14:45:45

7e008136-780a-4aed-8936-c1d053d78535R03